Heaven - The Final Destination!

Pathways for Catholics to Achieve Heaven

By Red O'Laughlin

Copyright © 2022 MRO Global, LLC

All rights reserved. No part of this book may be reproduced in any form or by electronic or mechanical means, including an information storage and retrieval system, without permission in writing from the publisher, except by a reviewer who may quote brief passages in a review.

Disclaimer. This book is educational. It is not intended as a substitute for the religious advice of your parish priests and the Catholic Church. Any errors or misinterpretations are attributed to the author alone.

ISBN: 9798326855534

First Edition: May 2024

MRO Global LLC Publisher

Red@redolaughlin.com, Red.Olaughlin@gmail.com

https://www.redolaughlin.com

Dedication Page

This book is dedicated to my parents (Red & Margaret O'Laughlin, now deceased) and all Catholics, especially practicing Catholics.

Table of Contents

Introduction 1

Catholic Doctrine & History 7

Pathways & Promises 11

Sacred Tradition 27

Definitions 35

About the Author - Personal 43

About the Author - Business 47

Introduction

I am not an authority on any aspect of Catholic Doctrine. I am a researcher. I investigate and analyze the chemical reactions in the human body at the cellular level looking for cause-and-effect relationships. Treat a cause and fix a problem. Treat symptoms and you will always be treating symptoms.

A few months ago, my mind was focusing on heaven – not only on how I can get to heaven but more importantly, how I can get to heaven bypassing purgatory. I put on my researcher hat and began the process of exploring the existing literature about heaven and the pathways to get there.

We are not privy to God's plans for us. We have His guidance and, with faith, live our lives in Christ and expect our final reward to be heaven. However, for most of us, purgatory is a stop before reaching heaven. Are there ways to bypass purgatory?

I have several Bibles, but the Douay-Rheims Bible is my preferred. I believe Jesus Christ came to earth and gave his life to expiate all sin and our salvation.

https://www.catholic.com/magazine/online-edition/did-jesus-have-to-die-for-us

He also gave us our Catholic religion by the words found in **Matthew 16:18-19 – 18** And I say to thee: That ***thou art Peter***; and ***upon this rock,*** I will build my church, and ***the gates of hell*** shall not prevail against it. **19** And I will give to thee the keys of the kingdom of heaven. And whatsoever thou shalt bind upon earth, it shall be bound also in heaven: and whatsoever thou shalt ***loose upon earth***, it shall be loosed also in heaven.

So, I needed to find statements made by God, Jesus Christ, the Holy Ghost, and Mary that have been evaluated and approved by Catholic Doctrine, Sacred Tradition, or Sacred Scripture. Catholic Doctrine teaches us that we can only enter heaven when all temporal punishment for our sins is removed through cleansing in purgatory. Are there options that we can take here on earth before our death that give us some assurance that if we comply with God's guidance, we have a reasonable expectation of heaven without purgatory?

Some subjects can be researched with certainty over time – chemistry, physics, and mathematics are a few. Some, like relationships, marriage, grieving, and religion cannot be as easily clarified. Nevertheless, we can make assumptions about what is true, what is false, and what we do not know.

As a religious disclaimer, we will never know with 100% assurance that the promises described in this book increase our chances of gaining heaven directly. I believe that most practicing Catholics will end up in Purgatory upon their death and eventually gain heaven. That is my personal belief.

I have been to many retreats over the years. I look forward to them. It is a chance for continual (and updated) learning. Several years ago, Father Larry Richards (https://www.thereasonforourhope.org/meet-father-larry/) gave a Lenten Retreat at my parish. One of the first questions he asked was about how we know people go to heaven. A little audience participation was generated and Fr. Larry spent half of the first night of the Retreat talking about how we can improve our chances of gaining heaven for our eternal reward.

Ask a priest (or Google it) 'What do I have to do to go to heaven?' The generic answer is to repent, have faith, and be baptized. https://www.catholic.com/magazine/online-edition/how-to-go-to-heaven. Heaven is a gift (salvation) we earn from God based on the Redemption Christ won on the Cross. None of us deserve it. We are free to accept or reject it.

What does the Catholic Church teach us about our journey after death? Immediately after death, our soul separates from our body, and we stand in judgment before God. Three options await us – immediately. Heaven, Purgatory, or Hell.

https://www.allentowndiocese.org/catholic-life/catholic-q/what-happens-us-after-we-die.

Very few enter heaven directly. The majority destined for heaven are sent to purgatory to be purified before entering heaven. Hell, however, is for those who willingly choose to reject God.

http://www.scborromeo.org/ccc/para/1022.htm. At the Last Judgment (at the End of Time – The Resurrection of the Dead) all souls will be joined with their bodies for a public judgment reflecting God's goodness and generosity. This 'second' judgment reinforces the judgment made immediately after death and provides final adjudication of those remaining souls to eternal salvation in heaven or ceaseless damnation in hell. https://www.catholic.com/magazine/online-edition/why-are-there-two-judgments

So, my research about how we can gain heaven without purgatory began. Sermons and homilies in the past couple or more decades have avoided the topics of heaven, hell, and purgatory. Why? I do not know. Maybe these topics were covered by other parishes, and I was unaware of them. I have been to several Retreats when these topics were touched on, but not in the detail I wanted.

I discovered immediately that asking Google or other AI (artificial intelligence) sources to list ways for me to gain heaven without purgatory does not work. I have seen the same thing in my research when asking Google or AI about health and wellness questions, such as, what causes Alzheimer's or cancer – the details are not available from a generic question.

I must approach the subject as if I already have an answer and need more detail. For example, tell me about uric acid and Alzheimer's disease. I can get a satisfactory answer to that type of question. So, I must find what promises have been made by God, Jesus, the Holy Ghost, and Mary over time that give us guidance to minimize our stay in purgatory or give us that extra boost straight into heaven.

Please enjoy. As I mentioned in my Dedication, this book is primarily for practicing Catholics. Everyone is welcome to the awareness and education provided herein, but please consult your parish religious authority for clarity. Any errors or misinterpretations of Catholic theology, Sacred Tradition, and Sacred Scripture are mine alone.

Catholic Doctrine & History

Again, I have no authority on this subject. I never had any formal education from the Catholic Church that helped me answer the basic question of, 'How do I get to heaven without going to purgatory?'

Why would or should I believe what the Catholic Church teaches? It is a fair question, even for Catholics. I was taught the Baltimore Catechism from my earliest memories of learning my faith. There was nothing to counter any statement that was made. It was given to me, and I accepted it, hook, line, and sinker – 100%.

However, as life passed by, my interest in learning more about many aspects of my life began to make itself present. At that time, I wanted someone to spoon-feed it to me. I was not willing or able to research things for myself.

For several years before the pandemic, my parish had summer movies (mostly with a religious theme) and educational studies on the Catholic Church. One such educational experience was about the first five hundred years of the Catholic Church after Jesus' death.

The first couple hundred years (A.D.) saw the Catholic Church grow a little, but by 300 A.D., Catholics numbered in the millions. Schisms, heresies, discord, dissent, conflict, and division were poking and prodding the beliefs established by Jesus Christ.

The best and the brightest at that time convened and began a vetting process to prove or disprove the tenets and future doctrine of our Catholic faith. Wikipedia lists dozens of schisms attacking Christianity over the centuries.

https://en.wikipedia.org/wiki/Schism_in_Ch ristianity

In the 300s, the scholars and church authorities convened an ecumenical council in Nicaea, Türkiye by the Roman Emperor Constantine.
https://www.britannica.com/event/First-Council-of-Nicaea-325 The first vetting of the Catholic Church occurred. What did we believe? Why did we believe it? What proof and physical evidence existed to support belief or disbelief?

Many manuscripts from different languages were analyzed, compared, and contrasted to show the whys and wherefores. This early vetting process and subsequent publication of the doctrines of the Catholic faith stuck with me – more so than my earlier religious training – now there was some evidence for what I believed.

I research Google, the Bible, religious articles, books, documentaries, and other virtual sources for awareness and education. The pandemic pushed virtual training and YouTube became a major interest in my education. Bishop Robert Barron, Msgr. Charles Pope, Fr. Larry Richards, Fr. Chad Ripperger, and others provided awareness and education about my Catholic faith.

I find amazing information about the Church, its teachings, and history, and wonder why I have never heard of these things before. Most likely, I was in the wrong place at the wrong time – or things were occurring, and they did not register in my life at that time. There are many reasons, but once I found a viable source, I gleaned it for added information repeatedly.

10

Pathways & Promises

What has the Catholic Church promised us through our LORD Jesus Christ and His Mother Mary that could allow our souls to enter heaven directly without a pit stop in purgatory?

Avoiding purgatory and entering heaven does not happen by accident.

https://www.ewtn.com/catholicism/library/how-to-avoid-purgatory-12562 . We must do things consciously to achieve our expectations. I use the word expectations since it directly communicates with our subconscious mind – the controller of our actions. 'Wants' and 'needs' address our conscious brain which controls extraordinarily little of our life.

Ask & Receive

Ask and you shall receive. Douay Rheims **Matthew 7.7**

https://www.drbo.org/chapter/47007.htm#:~:text=7%20Ask%2C%20and%20it%20shall,he%20reach%20him%20a%20stone%3F I prefer the Douay-Rheims Bible. Many

Catholics prefer a modern version, such as, the New American Bible, Saint Joseph Edition.

Are we asking God for a 'happy and holy' death daily? How about asking God 'to gain heaven without purgatory?' They are simple prayers we can ask daily (or more often). Ask and you shall receive!

Asking and receiving is not a promise, per se. God's response to our requests may never be known. Sometimes, the right answer is no answer – or not now.

I am not one to quote scripture and choose the Bible verses applicable to situations in life, nor will it be for this book. Some scripture references will be given, but it is not intended to be the norm. Most of us have access to a bible and can search/find what we seek from scripture, tradition, and magisterium. https://www.corpuschristiphx.org/blog?mont h=202008&id=1012135831&cat=93166170 8#:~:text=Today%2C%20we'll%20take%20 a,passing%20on%20of%20the%20Faith.&te xt=Catholics%20absolutely%20believe%20i n%20and%20respect%20the%20authority% 20of%20Sacred%20Scripture. Let us look at the sacraments and how they can help us gain heaven without purgatory.

Baptism (Sacrament)

What about the sacraments? Dying immediately after Baptism grants the baptized full pardon of all sins and instantaneous entry into heaven. Most of us are baptized as infants and it is no longer an option in our later years.

This is a viable option to gain heaven without purgatory for those who were never baptized and have that option on their deathbed.

Last Rites (Sacrament)

When my goal is to gain heaven without purgatory, one sacrament becomes paramount. I have known about this sacrament all my life but did not realize its true benefit for my soul at death until Fr. Larry Richards shouted it from the alter of my church during a Retreat – Extreme Unction or the Last Rites, or the Anointing of the Sick.

Usually with two other sacraments, Confession (Reconciliation) and Holy Communion, the Apostolic Pardon given to the priest administering Last Rites grants a

plenary indulgence for the total (full) remission of the temporal punishment of sin. Unlike a normal plenary indulgence, the Apostolic Pardon can be granted on the same day as a plenary indulgence (more on that shortly).
https://www.ncregister.com/features/apostolic-pardon-brings-total-forgiveness-before-death

When the time comes as our bodies are approaching the grave, it is wise to ask for Last Rites. There are many aspects of this sacrament and for those who want to know more, I suggest this link.

https://www.catholic.com/encyclopedia/extreme-unction.

This option, Last Rites, gives us a reasonable guarantee to gain heaven without purgatory. Do not leave your mortal life without it!

Divine Mercy Sunday

Going to Confession and receiving Holy Communion at the Divine Mercy mass grants the penitent a full (Feast of Mercy) plenary indulgence equal to that received by Baptism.
https://www.ewtn.com/catholicism/library/in

dulgences-attached-to-divine-mercy-devotions-1963

Divine Mercy Sunday allows Catholics to renew their Baptismal graces through a special plenary indulgence that eradicates the temporal punishment due to sin. So, once a year, Catholics can reset their spiritual meters back to zero with full participation in the sacraments while celebrating the Feast of Mercy on Divine Mercy Sunday.

This is definitely a viable option to consider – more so to reset the clock annually unless you are on your deathbed during the Easter Season.

Plenary Indulgence

Indulgences are granted by the church to remove fully or partially the temporal punishment associated with forgiven sins. We sin and go to confession and those sins are forgiven. Pretty simple, except.

The example I see used most often is the broken window. I am playing baseball in my yard. I hit a ball through a neighbor's window and broke it. The neighbor forgives me – and says, do not do it again! However, forgiveness is obtained, but the damage has not been repaired. That repair damage (temporal punishment) must be atoned for either through an indulgence or time spent in purgatory being purified.

https://www.usccb.org/sites/default/files/flip books/catechism/372/#zoom=z Our Catechism gives the basic description of indulgences. Prayers, actions, and other associated activities can qualify for a partial indulgence or a full or plenary indulgence according to the Enchiridion of Indulgences. https://www.catholic.org/prayers/indulgw.ph p

When I was much younger, I would see prayers with indulgence time associated with each prayer. One prayer might earn you three hundred days of indulgence when said. Another might yield seven years, seven months, and seven days. In 1968, that world changed, and indulgence reward (and definition) can be found in the Enchiridion of Indulgences.

A plenary indulgence is rewarded when the penitent goes to Confession, receives Communion, completes the plenary indulgence act, offers prayers for the Supreme Pontiff, is in total and complete detachment from sin, and the Apostle's Creed to confirm the existence of God. https://www.olpparish.com/uploads/3/2/2/5/32258261/plenary_indulgences_for_the_common_person.pdf

One wonderful thing about gaining plenary indulgences is that Confession can be done twenty days in advance or after the indulgence. The other aspects of indulgences are usually within a noticeably brief time of each other.

I can offer an indulgence for myself only – no other live person - or for a person who has died. Only one plenary indulgence can be granted daily. When a loved one has passed on without the Last Rites, consider doing a plenary indulgence for their soul to release them from purgatory so they can gain heaven more quickly.

This promise has some level of guarantee associated with it. For the deceased, it provides a shortened time in purgatory. For us living, we need to apply plenary indulgences for ourselves regularly.

First Fridays

St. Margaret Mary Alacoque had visions of the Sacred Heart of Jesus. Her visions became the nine First Friday's devotion that we observe – mass and communion for reparation of sins against the Sacred Heart of Jesus.

https://catholicmessenger.net/2024/03/question-box-first-friday-devotion-indulgence-explained/

There are many promises made to those completing the devotional requirements for nine First Fridays.

https://borgiaparish.org/first-fridays-devotion#:~:text=%E2%80%9CGreat%20Promise%E2%80%9D%3A-,%E2%80%9CI%20promise%20you%2C%20in%20the%20excessive%20mercy%20of%20my%20Heart,Heart%20shall%20be%20their%20safe

The last of the twelve promises for completing nine First Fridays is one in which our LORD stated that He would grant the grace of perseverance – that those completing this devotion would not die in disgrace without receiving their sacraments. If this implies Last Rites, I have touched on that subject already. Moreover, Jesus additionally said that His Divine Heart would be a safe refuge in our last moment.

Is this a guarantee that we skip purgatory and enter Heaven if we complete nine First Fridays as they are intended to be done? No, of course not. But there is nothing stipulating that it is not untrue. We might have completed the nine First Fridays devotional twenty years ago. Our lives change – especially as we have kids, new jobs, retire, and grow older. However, when we are serious about gaining heaven as our final destination, every little bit helps.

One day each month is difficult. I have tried it more than once and got sidetracked. It was not until recently that I completed the nine First Friday's devotion.

This promise is not as explicit as some of the others previously mentioned, but it does imply a link between death and heaven without purgatory – though not explicitly.

First Saturday

About the same time as World War I, Our Lady of Fatima requested Lucia that she would assist Lucia and others at their hour of death with the graces necessary for salvation. https://borgiaparish.org/first-saturdays-devotion

This devotion requires just a bit more than the First Friday devotion. Confession, Holy Communion, mass on the first Saturdays of five consecutive months, recital of the rosary, fifteen minutes of reflection on the mysteries of the rosary, and to make reparations to Mary.

There is no explicit promise of heaven while bypassing purgatory. However, there is a promise of the graces necessary to transition from our earthly bodies to our souls in heaven. Again, a promise that helps us immensely upon death.

Brown Scapular

The traditional promise for the wearer of the brown scapular is not to suffer eternal fire. This promise was initiated nearly a thousand years ago at Aylesford, England when Mary handed St. Simon Stock (a Carmelite) a brown, woolen scapular and promised those wearing it at their death would be spared from going to hell for the rest of their lives. Initially, the promise was made to only the Carmelite Order. A few decades later, the Catholic Church extended Mary's promise to all wearers of the brown scapular.

An interesting story about the brown scapular happened when Pope John Paul II was about to undergo surgery after the assassination attempt on his life, he demanded that his brown scapular not be removed during the pending surgery. Another interesting aspect about the brown scapular is that the rosary was introduced about the same time – 1200s.

I have worn the brown scapular for decades and observed how easy it is to break the cord. I tied the ends about one-quarter of an inch from the brown wool. I make a tight knot on both ends of the scapular. Pull as hard as you want the scapular will not come apart. Pulling on the knot protects the separation of the brown scapular material from the cord from separating.

Again, we do not have an explicit promise of entering heaven while bypassing purgatory. Nonetheless, protection from the eternal fires of hell is a good promise at the end of your life.

Seven Sorrows

Another important event happened in the 1200s – a newly formed Order of the Sorrows of Mary began a chaplet dedicated to the seven sorrows of Mary, the Mother of God. This devotion has been expanded into the Seven Sorrows Rosary and both are in active use today.

Two promises were made to those honoring the Seven Sorrows of Mary. One promise is her direct intervention at your time of death and grace from her Son. Mary will be visibly present when taking your last breaths. Mary's second promise from her Son, Jesus, is that those who propagate the Seven Sorrows devotion will be taken directly from this earthly life to eternal happiness.

That last promise sounds like you would not have the opportunity to wave at purgatory on the way to heaven.

https://www.ewtn.com/catholicism/seasons-and-feast-days/our-lady-of-sorrows-14632

St. Bridgit of Sweden

The promises associated with St. Bridgit are extraordinary. Our LORD made two promises to St. Bridgit. The first promise is to pray fifteen prayers daily for a year. The second promise is to pray seven prayers daily for twelve years. St. Bridgit lived in the 14th century and experienced many visions of our LORD.

She wanted to know how many blows our LORD had received during His Passion. Jesus appeared to her in Rome's Church of St. Paul while she was praying a rosary in front of a crucifix. Jesus told her that he had received 5,475 wounds – and, that fifteen Our Fathers and fifteen Hail Marys prayed every day for a year would equal 5,475.

There are additional prayers that were given to St. Bridgit to accompany fifteen recitations of the Our Father and Hail Mary. The truly astounding part of completing this devotion is the lengthy list of promises our LORD made to St. Bridgit.

https://www.theworkofgod.org/Devotns/brid get.htm

Yes, there are explicit promises of gaining heaven upon your death when you have completed the fifteen prayers of St. Bridgit every day for a year. The promises extend to your lineage. Over twenty promises are made to those completing this year-long prayer devotion.

My wife and I did this devotion together several years ago. It was not easy. I am doing them again by myself and it takes fifteen minutes of concentrated effort to complete all fifteen prayers daily.

But WAIT! There's MORE!

How about praying a devotional prayer daily for twelve years? Yes, twelve years. The promises are equal to the fifteen daily prayers done for a year.

https://stfrancisnewtonparish.com/the-12-year-prayers-by-st-bridget/

Our LORD promised St. Bridgit that praying the seven daily prayers for twelve years would exempt them from Purgatory. They will enter heaven and be accepted as martyrs. Additional promises address their lineage.

Others?

Are there other ways to get to heaven bypassing purgatory? I do not know. These are the ones easily found in my research. I am certain more exist.

Personal Plan

Everyone should have a personal plan on how to get to heaven. Keeping the sacraments is something that practicing Catholics do. However, ensure that family members know that you want Last Rites when the end of your life is imminent. Offer a plenary indulgence for yourself periodically. Wear the brown scapular. Complete the Nine First Fridays and the Five First Saturdays.

Offer every mass for the holy souls in purgatory – it never hurts! Take advantage of Divine Mercy Sunday each year. Seriously consider Mary's Seven Sorrows and St. Bridgit's prayers.

26

Sacred Tradition

Our Sacred Tradition is a source of Divine Truth and the foundation of the Catholic Church. The sacraments of Last Rites and Baptism are codified in Catholic Catechism. Likewise, indulgences are defined and described in the Catholic Catechism.

The Divine Mercy Sunday's apostolic indulgence is based on private discussions St. Faustina Kowalska had with our LORD. Pope John Paul II created the title in 2000 at the canonization of St. Faustina. This I believe falls more into the category of Sacred Tradition.

Angels and devils are included in the Catholic Catechism. As I delved into several exorcists and their firsthand experiences with Satan and his fellow devils, more details opened that are not fully clarified in our Catholic Catechism. Many exorcists have conversations with Satan or other devils during an exorcism. Historical findings uncovered by exorcists during discussions with devils are not fully vetted by the

Catholic Church. However, sometimes this information is made available to the public.

Fr. Chad Ripperger is a Catholic priest authorized to perform exorcisms. https://www.youtube.com/watch?v=wvB8k_ABjto and

https://www.youtube.com/watch?v=GMUjC8YRB5I are two interviews of Fr. Chad Ripperger and his insights into the diabolical influences within our world.

The devil is working overtime to take our salvation away from us by making us sin. It is a constant battle to fight an invisible, potent force that wants our souls in hell. The LORD's Prayer states, 'deliver us from evil.' Evil exists – everywhere. This reason alone makes me believe many will spend time in purgatory purging their transgressions to achieve the purity to enter heaven.

Exorcists can have conversations with devils. God allows that to happen. God has also allowed visions and apparitions to occur over the centuries. Catholic Catechism defines an apparition as the appearance of a heavenly being with people on earth.

My wife and I walked the Camino de Santiago in 2016. I learned during that pilgrimage that Mary, the Mother of Jesus Christ appeared to St. James around 40 A.D. in Spain and is regarded as the first apparition. Our LORD could multiply loaves and fishes and reignite life into those dead for days. Why is it a stretch to believe that visions and apparitions are not part of our Sacred Tradition?

There have been nearly four hundred visions and apparitions investigated by the Catholic Church. Only eight have been recognized by the Catholic Church, twenty-five by local bishops, and sixteen by the Vatican. Most Catholics recognize Rue du Bac (France), La Salette (France), Lourdes (France), Fatima (Portugal), Akita (Japan), and Kibeho (Rwanda) as Marian apparitions.

Yet, hundreds of other visions have occurred that have not been fully approved. I have been to Medjugorje, Bosnia-Herzegovina twice and when asked about the Catholic Church's adoption of that apparition as true, the standard answer is that it takes time. OK, I understand – do not jump into something without the absolute total agreement of everyone involved in making that decision in the Catholic Church's name.

What about miracles? The Catholic Catechism also determines the validity of miracles – a sign or wonder, such as healing, or control of nature, which can only be attributed to Divine Power.

Our LORD performed dozens of miracles during his time in life. Is there any reason why His Power cannot be manifested through mortal beings on earth? We pray to God for a miracle and sometimes it is granted. We pray to the Saints and see comparable results – prayers granted that can be classified as miracles.

Other times, family or friends pray for a miracle for us. Still, in some unique situations, God grants miracles that no one prayed for.

https://www.ncregister.com/blog/the-jesuit-priests-who-survived-hiroshima#:~:text=Four%20of%20the%20priests%20whose,hearing%20loss%20from%20the%20explosion. Jesuit priests were saved during the atomic bombing of Hiroshima.

The atomic bomb blast leveled the city. Several Jesuit priests survived without any radiation sickness, hearing, or vision issues for decades after WW II. God also spared several Catholic clergies caught in the blast radius of Nagasaki.

https://www.chicagocatholic.com/chicagoland/-/article/2022/10/05/catholic-atomic-bomb-survivors-from-nagasaki-share-personal-stori-1

A Lebanese monk, Youssef Antown Makhlouf, was elevated to sainthood as St. Charbel. God has his favorites on earth as we do. The link below claims more than 33,000 miracles granted in St. Charbel's name (also spelled Sharbel). I have seen claims of over 80,000 miracles during my research on St. Charbel.

https://www.familyofsaintsharbel.org/miracles.html

Miracles attributed to St. Charbel have been documented in over 133 countries from various religions including Christians, Muslims, Buddhists, Hindus, Jews, Druze, Alawites, and Atheists.

So, God, Jesus Christ, the Holy Ghost, and Mary are attributed with visions, apparitions, and miracles. I believe there have been communications with specific Saints that provide guidance for us to gain heaven – and some that provide a bypass of purgatory.

Similarly, miracles are granted to those who pray for them. Not every prayer is answered with a miracle. God's will be done! However, we do have some tools in our arsenal to help us battle demons that want to control our souls.

Fr. Jim Blount, SOLT (Society of Our Lady of the Trinity) passed away in late 2023. He is well known for a twelve-word deliverance prayer – *"Most Precious Blood of Jesus Christ, Save us and the Whole World."* Additionally, miracles, healings, and conversions attributed to him are numerous. https://www.youtube.com/watch?v=jQIHEIGtro8

I had a DIY (Do It Yourself) double bypass on my heart a while back when my left descending anterior artery became clogged. I view Fr. Blount's twelve-word deliverance prayer as a powerful tool to drive away Satan and other demons – a DIY exorcism of sorts. Sometimes, possession by a demon is manifested in ways we never thought could happen. Deliverance prayers help us and those we love to break the barrier that prevents us from living our lives in Christ.

https://catholicexchange.com/vexation-obsession-possession-the-extraordinary-ways-the-devil-attacks/

Paul Harvey, an American radio broadcaster did a dramatic expose on the devil. I am certain many of you have heard it.

https://www.ilfop.org/if-i-were-the-devil-by-paul-harvey/

34

Definitions

Please note that the definitions given in this chapter refer specifically to Catholic Doctrine and provide a quick reference.

Apparitions

A supernatural appearance by Mary and Jesus to a person or group of people

Apostolic Pardon

The blessing and indulgence given to the dying to remove all punishment associated with sin.

Angels

Immortal and spiritual servants and messengers of God with intelligence and will

Baptism

A Christian sacrament using water to initiate a person into public and personal identification with Jesus and the Christian community.

Brown Scapular

A Roman Catholic devotion to Mary, the Mother of Jesus using a brown woolen piece of cloth worn around the neck.

Confession (Reconciliation)

A Catholic Church sacrament uses a verbal recital of sins to a priest and acknowledges our sinful nature specifically to gain mercy from God.

Deliverance Prayers

A prayer to God, the angels, or saints asking for freedom from the power of the devil.

Devils

The personification of evil by a fallen angel seeking constant opposition to God

Divine Mercy Sunday

The first Sunday after Easter is when God provides his mercy to those struggling with sin and despair.

Doctrine

Universal teachings and beliefs of the Catholic Church

Ecumenical Council

An official meeting of Catholic bishops, cardinals, and prelates overseen by the pope to settle doctrinal disputes.

Exorcize

A process used by a priest to drive away evil spirits from a person or place.

Extreme Unction (Last Rites)

A Catholic sacrament is used to help injured people recover and for the salvation of those near death.

Faith

A theological virtue whereby a person believes in one, true, living God.

Final Resurrection

The time when our bodies and souls will be reunited as one.

First Fridays

A devotion and practice of receiving Holy Communion on the first Friday of every month for nine consecutive months to honor the Sacred Heart of Jesus

First Saturdays

A devotion and practice of receiving Holy Communion on the first Saturday of five consecutive months to honor the Immaculate Heart of Mary

Heaven

The attainment of supreme happiness with a beatific vision of God forever

Hell

A permanent separation from God and his mercy

Heresy

A denial or doubt of a Catholic truth or doctrine

Indulgence

Extra-sacramental graces extended to remit temporal punishment associated with forgiven sin.

Magisterium

The official authority of the Catholic Church guided by the Holy Spirit

Mortal Sin

A serious action committed with full knowledge of its gravity and deliberate consent.

Near Occasion of Sin

A situation that can lead to temptation but is not sinful.

Pardon for Sins

The forgiveness of sin

Plenary Indulgence

The complete remission of the temporal punishment associated with forgiven sins.

Prayers

A spiritual practice of worship or communication with God

Promise

A binding vow

Purgatory

A temporary state for the purification of souls from the temporal punishment of their sins that prepares them to enter heaven. Purgatory is not explicitly mentioned in the Bible but is included in the Catechism of the Catholic Church (CCC 1030-1032)

Sacrament

A sign of grace instituted by Jesus, entrusted to the Catholic Church to dispense divine life.

Schism

A willful refusal to submit to the Holy Pontiff and unity of the Catholic Church

Scripture

A collection of sacred books containing the inspired word of God

Seven Sorrows

A devotion to the seven events of Mary's life that caused Her extreme duress.

St. Bridgit of Sweden

Patron saint of Sweden and founder of the Order of the Most Holy Savior

Temporal Punishment

The consequences of sin remaining after forgiveness.

Tradition

The teachings of Jesus and the Apostles passed down by word of mouth.

Venial Sin

Something immoral but not gravely immoral and not a rejection of God

Visions

A prophetic or supernatural image in which our mind receives an extraordinary grasp of a revealed truth without the aid of our senses

About the Author - Personal

I am a cradle Catholic and the oldest of nine children. My parents, Francis Michael (Red) O'Laughlin, Jr. and Margaret Mae (White) O'Laughlin were dedicated practicing Catholics. We went to mass every Sunday and took up the entire left front row of the church. My father was in the military and retired when I was in my early teens. We moved every year-and-a-half to two years.

I went to Catholic school in the fourth grade and again for four years of high school. During my last couple of years of college, my family moved to California. I stayed in Corpus Christi, TX to finish college. I got married, graduated from college, joined the military, and got an invitation to Vietnam.

After several training assignments, I became a Naval Aviator, like my father. My wife, Marilyn, delivered our first child, Michelle, while I was training in San Diego. Shortly thereafter, I went to my first active-duty command in Hawaii and experienced several deployments in the Western Pacific (Philippines, Vietnam, Thailand, and

Okinawa) flying Vietnam Market Time operations in the Western Pacific Ocean, the South China Sea, and the Indian Ocean.

Overseas, my usual twelve-hour missions occasionally ended up taking off from one country and landing in another. Trying to keep a weekly Sunday mass was impossible. My deployments were around six months.

In Hawaii, our second was born, our son. We attended weekly mass and grew incrementally in our faith through the remainder of my time on active duty. We left Hawaii, assumed residence in California with my first civilian job, and joined the Reserves (flying anti-submarine missions for the next dozen years). Red's last two years were on active duty in support of operations in Bosnia.

Decades ago, in my forties, I was frustrated with several things going on in my spiritual life. My father happened to be sitting nearby and I broached the subject with him. The best advice, absolutely the best advice I ever received from my father was – "Do not confuse the church with the administration!" People are people and they have egos and agendas, and they may not always be aligned with the precepts and doctrines of the Catholic faith. Instantly, a light bulb went on in my brain and I was easily able to separate administration from the tenets of my faith.

My first of five academic degrees was in chemistry. I never practiced as a chemist because of the invitation to Vietnam. I spent thirty-one-plus years in the military with most of that in the Reserves.

I use my chemistry degree nowadays to research the human body at the cellular level looking for cause-and-effect relationships – chemically speaking. Treat a cause and fix a problem! Treat symptoms and you will always treat symptoms – and, sometimes, the underlying cause continues to grow and become worse.

I have always had a yearning to learn (additionally, I have seven professional certifications). When my wife developed breast cancer, I dusted off my chemical knowledge to research how to attack the various side effects she was having from chemotherapy (and most of them worked).

46

About the Author - Business

F. M. 'Red' O'Laughlin was a Naval Flight Officer and retired as a Captain with 31 years in the Navy Reserves. He is one of the most successful antisubmarine tacticians and has nearly one thousand flights in P3 aircraft. Red has traveled to sixty+ countries. He has written over a thousand documents (policies, procedures, instructions, flow charts, etc.) in his career. Additionally, he has written over a thousand original content articles on health and wellness posted on LinkedIn.

His civilian specialties are quality assurance, reliability engineering, and logistics. He has worked in senior management positions at National Semiconductor, Memorex, Dresser Industries, NL Industries, Boeing, and Halliburton. He has an A.A. in Quality Assurance from De Anza College, a B.S. in Chemistry from Texas A&I, an M.S. in Systems Management from U.S.C., an M.B.A. in International Business from the University of Houston, and a graduate of the Naval War College. He has been certified as an ISO-9000 Assessor and Evaluator, TapRooT Assessor, Distinguished

Toastmaster, Certified Quality Engineer, Certified Reliability Engineer, Quality Manager, and Certified Professional Logistician. Red has authored seven books.

Red has been associated with the Knights of Columbus since he was a teenager and has held the positions of Grand Knight, Faithful Navigator, and District Deputy in the Houston-Galveston area.

Red is a researcher and regularly authors articles and blogs on health, nutrition, and self-improvement. Red can be reached at red.olaughlin@gmail.com. Red's website is https://www.RedOLaughlin.com. Red has been married to Marilyn for 56 years (in July 2024), and they have two children, three grandchildren, and one great-grandson.

Red also hosts or co-hosts several live-streaming weekly television shows on the USA Global Television & Radio Network. He loves to read, cook, garden, and travel. This is his first book on the Catholic Church. Red and his wife, Marilyn, walked the Camino de Santiago in 2016 completing the five-hundred-mile pilgrimage in thirty days.

ALSO, BY F. M. 'RED' O'LAUGHLIN

No Matter What You Can Do It:

The Ultimate Guide to Obtaining Whatever You Want in Life

Failure Is Not an Option:

Insider Secrets to Master Setting

And Achieving Your Goals

Longevity Secrets for Healthy Aging:

How to Live to One Hundred Years of Age with the Body of a Healthy 50-Year-Old and the Mind of a 25-Year-Old

The Joy of Ageless Health

How to be Healthy, Active, and Vibrant as You Age

Understanding the Causes of Alzheimer's Disease

The Essential New Author's Guide

A Comprehensive Checklist for Writing and Publishing Your Book on Time and on Budget

Made in the USA
Columbia, SC
05 June 2024

36307316R00030